More Mini Mathematical Murder Mysteries

16 Activities to stretch and engage ages 13-15

Jill Whieldon

tarquin

Publisher's Note

This is the second appearance of Jill Whieldon's Mini Mathematical Murder Mysteries, after the great popularity of the first volume. For more details, see below.

You can keep up to date with this and other new titles, special offers and more, through registering on our website for our e-mail newsletter or following us on Twitter or Facebook.

Other Titles in the Series

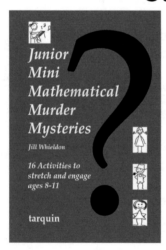

Junior Mini Mathematical Murder Mysteries
...for ages 8-11

and

More Mini Mathematical Murder Mysteries
...for ages 13-15

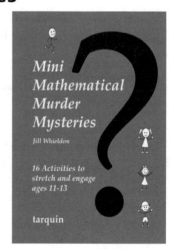

Published by Tarquin Publications
Suite 74, 17 Holywell Hill
St Albans
AL1 1DT

www.tarquingroup.com

Distributed in the USA by Parkwest
www.parkwestpubs.com
www.amazon.com & major retailers

Distributed in Australia by OLM
www.lat-olm.com.au

Copyright © Jill Whieldon, 2012
ISBN: 978-1-907550-25-6

Printed in the USA or Australia and designed in the United Kingdom

Introduction

We all like to think we can solve a murder given the right clues. Here's a chance to use mathematics skills to identify "whodunnit".

The topics covered in this book are all included in the year 8 and 9 schemes of work in mathematics, so are aimed at the 12-14 age group. The tasks have been used successfully with older pupils too as a reminder of topics covered previously.

They would also be suitable for younger pupils who have met the appropriate language and content. They are likely to take about 40 mins but this will depend on the ability of the class to coordinate the different aspects of each task.

The book is aimed at:

Teachers

The idea is to use this as consolidation rather than as a teaching tool. It's worked well with a variety of classes and I've always put the students in pairs to enable them to talk about the methods they're using while they solve the "murder". I've found that their cooperative skills have improved as has their ability to plan and delegate in a bid to "win". I'd suggest a practice run through of one of the "who" suspects the first time you use one of these mysteries to help the class in the organisation process.

Parents

Much more fun than having endless maths exercises to trawl through! Children will engage with the mathematics because it is presented here in an entertaining way. Make sure that your child does know what the key concepts are for each mystery before starting.

Thanks

Thanks must go to the pupils in my classes at Prince Henry's Grammar School who have trialled these activities and suggested names for the suspects. Many will find themselves on these pages.

I hope you and your children enjoy putting on your "detective's hats" and solving these mini murder mysteries.

Jill Whieldon

Mini Murder Mystery 17
Percentage mix

WHO?

The 6 suspects have each made 2 statements about the ages of the members of 3 families.

The victim has made 0 errors, the murderer has made 2 errors.

Family name	Aged 0 - 10	Aged 11- 20	Aged 21 - 40	Aged over 40
Williams	2	0	2	0
Jones	1	2	1	1
Smith	0	1	3	2

Josiah says
- 50% of the Williams family are aged 0-10
- 50% of the Smith family are over 40

Patrick says
- 40% of everyone is aged up to 20
- 50% of the children up to 10 are in the Jones family

Lydia says
- $33\frac{1}{3}$% of the Smith family are over 40
- $33\frac{1}{3}$% of the 11-20 year olds are in the Smith family

Hannah says
- 40% of the Jones family are aged 21-40
- The Smith family is 50% larger than the Williams family

Lucy says
- The Jones family is 20% larger than the Williams family
- 50% of everyone is aged 11-40

Greg says
- 25% of everyone is aged 21-40
- 20% of the Jones family are over 40

WHERE?

Sabeel invested £30 million in a bank bond. The same amount of interest was added each year. After 3 years the total had risen to £30.45million.
What annual % interest rate was the bank using ?

If the annual interest rate is 5% the murder happened at the bank.	If the annual interest rate is 0.5% the murder happened at the charity shop.
If the annual interest rate is 4.5% the murder happened at the exclusive ladieswear shop.	If the annual interest rate is 1.5% the murder happened at the Michelin starred restaurant.

 **WHEN?** This rectangle measures 28m by 15m. Its length is going to be increased by 25% and its width is going to be decreased by 20%.

Decide whether the 4 statements below are true or false to work out the time and date of the murder.

Statement	If true choose this	If false choose this
Its area will increase by 5%	5am	5pm
Its new length will be 35m	Saturday	Friday
Its new width will be 3m	9th July	5th March
The area will remain the same	2013	2014

 **WHY?** Work out the multiplier for each of these % increases or decreases then use your answers to decode the murderer's message.

A	C	E	F	H
20% increase	6% decrease	70% decrease	35% increase	60% increase
I	M	N	O	P
80% decrease	100% increase	65% decrease	6% increase	21% decrease
R	S	T	X	Y
79% increase	11% decrease	100% decrease	40% increase	30% decrease

0.89	1.6	0.3	1.2	0	0.3	0.89
0.2	1.4	0	0.7	0.79	0.3	1.79
0.94	0.3	0.35	0	1.06	1.35	2
0.7	0.94	1.6	0.2	0.79	0.89	

FINAL ACCUSATION

_____ murdered _____

At (place) _____ on (Date) _____

Because (why) _____

Mini Murder Mystery 18
Approximating & Rounding

WHO?

The 6 suspects have each made 3 statements about the 10 decimals below.

The murderer has made 3 errors, the victim 0 errors.

3.539	3.648	3.059	3.191	3.851
3.909	3.678	3.725	3.148	3.262

Tony says
- 2 of the numbers would round off to 3.6 (1 dec pl)
- None of the numbers round off to 3.0 (1 dec pl)
- 2 of the numbers round off to 3.9 (1 dec pl)

Christopher says
- 1 number rounds off to 3.1 (1 dec pl)
- The difference between the number that rounds to 3.5 and the one that rounds to 3.6 is 0.111
- None of the numbers round off to 3.4 (1 dec pl)

Philip says

- Half the numbers round off to 4 to the nearest integer
- 1 number rounds off to 3.8 (1 dec pl)
- Adding 0.01 to every number will alter what they all round off to

Lucy says

- 2 numbers round off to 3.2 (1 dec pl)
- The difference between the 2 numbers that round off to 3.9 is 0.059
- 1 number rounds off to 3.6 (1 dec pl)

Anne says
- The gap between the 2 numbers that round off to 3.1 is 0.087
- All the numbers would round off to 3 to the nearest integer
- 1 number rounds off to 3.2 (1 dec pl)

Janet says
- There are 7 different answers
- 3.8 is not one of the answers
- The difference between the 2 numbers that round off to 3.7 is 0.047

WHEN?

Which is the odd one out in each set of values? Write the digits of each answer below (ignore decimal points) to form the date and time of the murder. Write 1 digit per box.

Round them to 1 dec pl then decide.	29.18, 29.19, 28.92, 29.24, 29.21
Round to 2 dec pl then decide	0.119, 0.123, 0.121, 0.115, 0.125
Round to 1 sig fig then decide	4.5, 4.8, 4.3, 4.9, 5.3

date		month	year				hours		mins	

WHERE?

If any of these numbers does not round off to 4000 the murder took place in Winchester	4449 (nearest 1000) 3951 (nearest 100) 4449 (1 sig fig) 3999 (2 sig figs)
If any of these numbers does not round off to 250 the murder was in Southampton	248 (nearest 10), 230 (nearest 50), 254.88 (2 sig figs) 251.1 (nearest integer)
If any of these numbers does not round off to 100 the murder took place in Portsmouth	135.89 (1 sig fig) 54.03 (nearest 100) 103.5 (2 sig figs) 97.71(nearest 5)

WHY?

Round each number to 1 sig fig then calculate the approximate answer. Use the answer to decode the murderer's message. (eg for A. 6.41 +11.2 ≈ 6 + 10 = 16)

A	C	D	E	G
6.41 + 11.2	19.1 ÷ 2.11	108 x 0.52	36.9 - 18.7	465 ÷ 198
H	I	L	M	N
60.7 + 14.3	0.88 x 3.8	994 ÷ 220	91.57 - 48.88	0.066 x 98.3
O	P	S	T	U
67 ÷ 23.1	239 x 16.2	9.11 x 8.88	78 x 41.9	17 x 33.7

81	70	20	3200	70	3.5	600	2.5	70	3200	50
20	10	4000	5	40	20	16	7	3200	50	20
10	3.6	50	20	4000	5	20	16	81	20	

FINAL ACCUSATION

_____ murdered _____

On (when) _____ at (where) _____

Why_____

Mini Murder Mystery 19
Powers of 10

WHO?

Each of the suspects has made 3 statements.
The murderer has made 3 errors. The victim has made 0 errors.
The others have made 1 or 2 errors.

Becky says
- $24 \times 10 = 24 \div {}^1\!/_{10}$
- $3.6 \times 10^2 = 72$
- Half of 4.5 million is 2.25×10^5

Chris says
- $20 \times 1000 = 200 \times 100$
- $46 \times 0.001 = 46 \div 100$
- A quarter of 8×10^8 is 2×10^2

Adam says
- $8 \times 10^3 = 8 \div {}^1\!/_{1000}$
- $0.45 \times 1000 = 450$
- One twelfth of 6 million is 5×10^5

Alex says
- $0.6 \times 100 = 600 \div 100$
- $330 \times {}^1\!/_{100} = 0.33$
- 30 thousand $\div$ 300 is 10^3

Catherine says
- $10 \div {}^1\!/_{1000} =$ ten thousand
- $1.2 \times 10^2 = 2.4 \times 10$
- $3 \times 10^3 + 2 \times 10^3 = 5 \times 10^3$

Lena says
- $0.67 \times 10 = 67 \times 0.1$
- $5900 \times {}^1\!/_{10} = 59 \times 10$
- $4 \times 10^2 + 1 \times 10^3 = 4.1 \times 10^5$

WHERE?

Work out the answer to the following calculations. Then select the correct letters and unscramble them to reveal where the murder happened.

Calculate this	If the answer is > 10^2	If the answer is < 10^2
$(1.3 \times 10^2) - (0.2 \times 10)$	S	W
$(1.4 \times 10^3) - (1.35 \times 10^3)$	D	S
$(4.9 \times 10^3) \div (7 \times 10^2)$	O	W
$(6 \times 10^2) \div (5 \times 10)$	I	E
$(0.8 \times 10^2) - (0.15 \times 10^2)$	N	A
$(2 \times 10^2) - (0.9 \times 10)$	N	S
$(2.02 \times 10^2) \div 2$	A	N

 **WHEN?** Work out the 2 calculations below.
Then multiply the 2 answers and compare this final answer to the possible dates.

Two times one hundredth	Six divided by nought point nought one
0.12 means it was on Dec 12th 1912	120 means it was on Jan 20th 2000
12 means it was on Oct 10th 2010	1.2 means it was on 1st Feb 2001

 **WHY?** Calculate the answers for each letter then decode the message below

A	B	C	D	E
6×10^2	$3 \div 1000$	$21 \div 100$	4.5×10^2	3.8×100
F	**G**	**H**	**I**	**J**
$38 \div 0.01$	50×0.01	$3 \times 10 \div 100$	$6 \times {}^1/_{10}$	$2.1 \times {}^1/_{100}$
K	**L**	**M**	**N**	**O**
6×10^3	$6 \div 10^2$	$3 \div 100$	$0.3 \div {}^1/_{10}$	$45 \div 1000$
P	**Q**	**R**	**S**	**T**
$0.38 \div {}^1/_{10}$	$2 \times 100 \div {}^1/_{10}$	$0.2 \div {}^1/_{10}$	$3 \div {}^1/_{10}$	0.2×10^2
U	**V**	**W**	**X**	**Y or Z**
$0.6 \div 100$	$450 \div 100$	0.045×10^3	$10 \times 10 \times 10$	30×10

0.003	380	0.21	600	0.006	30	380	0.3
380	45	600	30	30	0.045	3.8	0.045
45	380	2	3800	0.006	0.06		

FINAL ACCUSATION

_____ murdered_____

On (when) _____ at (where) _____

Because (why)_____

Mini Murder Mystery 20
Standard Form

WHO?

Here are 4 numbers written in standard form. The 6 characters below have each made 2 statements about them. The murderer has made 2 errors and the victim has made 0 errors. The others made 1 error. No calculators

$A = 3 \times 10^4$	$B = 4 \times 10^5$	$C = 6 \times 10^{-2}$	$D = 1.2 \times 10^9$

Michael says

- $A + B = 3.4 \times 10^5$
- $C \div D = 5 \times 10^{-11}$

Jake says

- $C \times D = 7.2 \times 10^7$
- $D \div A = 4 \times 10^6$

Hollie says

- $B - A = 3.7 \times 10^4$
- $D \div A = B$

Sam says

- $A \times B \div D = 10$
- $C \div D = 5 \times 10^{-11}$

Catherine says

- $C \times B = 2.4 \times 10^4$
- $C \div B = 1.5 \times 10^3$

Beth says

- $B \times D = 4.8 \times 10^{14}$
- $C \div A = 2 \times 10^2$

WHEN?

Decide on the **largest** value in each row to establish the time and date of the murder

2.04 × 10⁶ means 4 mins past 2 pm	2 and ¼ million Means ¼ past 2 pm	259,000 Means 2:59 pm
6×10^{-4} Means 6th April	One thousandth Means 1st January	3.1×10^{-3} Means 31st March
2011×10^2 Means in 2011	0.2012×10^5 Means 2012	$20\ 100\ 000 \times 10^{-3}$ Means 2010

WHERE?

Because the moon follows an elliptical orbit its distance from the earth varies. Its average distance from earth is approx 3.84×10^5 km. If the closest it approaches earth is approx 364 000 km, what is its furthest distance? Match the answer to the place where the murder happened.

At a rugby match if it's 3.74×10^5 km

At an ice hockey match if it's 4.04×10^5 km

At a basketball game if it's 4×10^5 km

At a football match if it's 7.84×10^5 km

WHY?

Write these numbers in standard form, then decode the message from the murderer.

A	D	E	H	I	N	Q
265 000	26 500	0.265	265	256×10^{-1}	0.00256	25 600 000
R	S	T	U	W	Y	
0.256	265×10^{-2}	0.0256	25.6×10^5	2065	2056	

2.56×10^3	2.65×10^{-1}	2.65×10^0	2.65×10^5	2.56×10^1
2.65×10^4	2.56×10^{-2}	2.65×10^{-1}	2.56×10^{-3}	2.65×10^0
2.56×10^7	2.56×10^6	2.65×10^5	2.56×10^{-1}	2.65×10^{-1}
2.65×10^4	2.065×10^3	2.65×10^5	2.65×10^0	2.56×10^{-2}
2.065×10^3	2.65×10^{-1}	2.56×10^{-3}	2.56×10^{-2}	2.056×10^3

FINAL ACCUSATION

_____ murdered _____

At (place) _____ on (Date) _____ at(time)_____

Why_____

Mini Murder Mystery 21
Mixed Algebra

WHO?

These 6 suspects have each made 3 mathematical statements involving expanding a bracket or factorising. One of them has made no errors. This is the victim. One of them has made 3 errors. This is the murderer.

George says

- $3(6x + 2) = 18x + 5$
- $16(2x - 3) = 32x - 19$
- $24 - 36x = 12(2 - 3x)$

Amy says

- $5x + 5 = 5(x + 1)$
- $100 - 80x = 20(5 - 4x)$
- $8(3x + 2) = 24x + 16$

Lily says

- $2(6x - 2) = 12x - 4$
- $15x + 3 = 3(5x + 3)$
- $7x^2 + 21x = 7x(x + 21)$

Sam says

- $6x(10 + x) = 60x + 6x$
- $27 - 9x = 9(3x - 1)$
- $5(2x + 5) = 10x + 25$

Oliver says

- $4(6 - 7x) = 24 - 42x$
- $36x - 18 = 18(2x - 1)$
- $9x + 18 = 9(x + 9)$

Beth says

- $4(3x + 4) = 12x + 8$
- $x(x - 1) = 2x - 1$
- $50 + 16x = 66x$

WHEN?

Substitute the given x values into these expressions to find the possible times and dates for the murder. Then select the earlier time and the later date

	Time (hours) x^2	Time (mins) $5x$	Date (day) $10-x$	Date (month) $4(x-1)$
Use x = 3				
Use x = 4				

WHERE?

Here are 2 shapes with angles given as algebraic expressions. Beneath are equations for the sum of the interior angles of the 2 shapes.
The place of the murder is linked to the correct pair of equations.

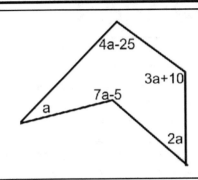

In the lounge if both these are correct	In the dining room if both these are correct
• $17a - 20 = 720$ • $b + c + d = 180$	• $17a = 540 + 20$ • $360 - b - c - d = 0$
In the kitchen if both of these are correct	In the bathroom if both these are correct
• $a + 4a + 3a + 2a + 7a + 10 - 25 - 5 = 360$ • $180 - (b + c + d) = 180$	• $a + 4a + 3a + 2a + 7a + 10 - 25 - 5 = 540$ • $180 + b + c + d = 180$

WHY?

Solve these equations to decode the murderer's confession.

A	C	E	G
$2x + 5 = x - 1$	$5x - 8 = 3x + 2$	$6x - 9 = 2x + 3$	$9x + 12 = 3x - 12$
H	I	L	N
$4x + 3 = 5x - 1$	$2x + 9 = 5x + 6$	$4x - 7 = 2x - 3$	$10x + 3 = 5x - 2$
O	R	S	T
$x + 8 = 3x - 8$	$4x - 17 = 6x - 1$	$3x + 9 = 2x$	$5x + 3 = 8x + 12$
U	W	X	Y
$6x + 1 = 5x + 1$	$6x + 4 = 5x + 2$	$8x + 30 = 4x + 10$	$5x = 3x + 12$

-9	4	3	-2	-8	8	-3	3	-6	-9
-3	-8	-6	1	-4	4	-3	-5	-1	8
-3	-6	5	0	-8	2	6	8	-1	3

FINAL ACCUSATION

_____ murdered _____

On (when) _____ at (where) _____

Because (why)_____

Mini Murder Mystery 22
Harder Sequences

 **WHO?**

Here are rules for 4 sequences. The 6 suspects have each made 3 statements about these sequences. The murderer has made 3 errors, the victim has made none.
(Hint: write down the first 5 terms of each sequence to help.)

Sequence 1 $nth term = \dfrac{n(n+1)}{2}$	Sequence 2 $n^{th} term = n^2 - 4$	Sequence 3 $nth term = \dfrac{n}{2} + \dfrac{(n-1)}{3}$	Sequence 4 $n^{th} term = \dfrac{n^2 + 4}{n}$

Lena
- All 4 are quadratic sequences
- Sequence 2 contains only square numbers
- The 3rd sequence is equivalent to (2n-1)/5

Harriet
- The first sequence is the triangular numbers
- The second sequence is the only one with a negative number in it
- There are no integers in sequence 3

Will
- Sequence 4 has equal differences
- The 2nd differences in sequence 1 are 2
- Sequence 3 is linear

Florence
- The 1st and 4th terms are equal in sequence 3
- The 2nd differences in sequence 2 are 2
- Sequence 1 is the same as $n^2 + \frac{1}{2}$

Ciaran
- Sequence 3 is equivalent to (5n – 2)/6
- The terms in sequence 4 decrease then increase
- 0 only appears in sequence 2

Max
- The terms in sequence 4 increase steadily
- The common difference in sequence 3 is 5/6
- Sequence 1 is quadratic

 **WHEN?**

Here are 4 statements about sequences.
Decide how many are true to find when the murder happened.

The sequence 5n - 4 will have a common difference of -4	The sequence $4n^2 - 3n$ will have 2nd differences of 8
A quadratic sequence with 2nd differences of 6 will have a rule starting with 12n^2	The sequence 20 – 4n will have a common difference of -4

If 1 is true it was 1st Jan 2001	If 2 are true it was 2nd Feb 2002
If 3 are true it was 3rd March 2003	If all 4 are true it was 4th April 2004

WHERE?	This sequence of overlapping circles shows the points of intersection. Decide which of the suggested rules is correct for the number of points to establish where the murder took place.

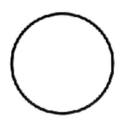
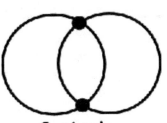
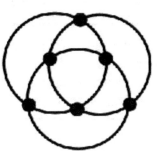
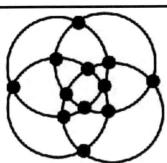

1 circle
0 points

2 circles
2 points

By the swings if it's	$2n - 2$	By the roundabout if it's	$n^2 - n$
By the slide if it's	$n^2 - 2n$	By the seesaw if it's	$2n - n$

WHY?	Calculate the 3rd term in each of these sequences then decode the murderers message

A	C	D	E	H	I
$n^2 - 3n$	$2n^2 - n$	$20 - 4n$	$\dfrac{(2n)^2}{3}$	$\dfrac{n}{2} + \dfrac{2n}{3}$	$100 - 9n^2$
N	Q	R	S	U	W
$\dfrac{n^2 + 9}{n}$	$\dfrac{12 - 2n}{2n}$	$5n + 3$	$\dfrac{2n^3 - 4}{n + 2}$	$(3n)^2$	$(\frac{1}{2}n)^2 + \frac{3}{4}$

3.5	12	10	0	19	8	10	12
1	81	12	5	15	12	10	3
12	18	12	3.5	0	18	8	

FINAL ACCUSATION

_____ murdered _____

On (date) _____ at (where) _____

Because (why)_____

Mini Murder Mystery 23
Straight Line Graphs

WHO?

One of the following 6 people has murdered one of the others.
Each has made 4 statements about these 2 graphs.
The murderer has made 3 errors, the victim made 0 errors.
The other suspects made 1 or 2 errors

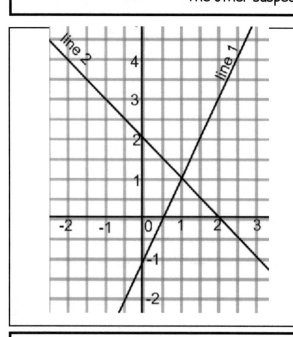

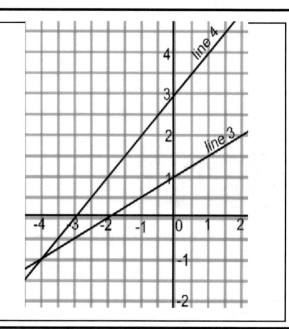

Lily says
- Line 1 is steeper than line 3
- Gradient of line 3 is 0.5
- (1,0) is on line 3
- (2,3) is on line 1

Chloe says
- The gradient of line 4 is 1
- The gradient of line 2 is -1
- The y intercept of Line 3 is 1
- (4,3) would be on line 3

Lucy says
- Lines 1 & 2 are perpendicular
- The gradient of line 4 is 3
- (0, -1) is on line 1
- Line 3 is steeper than line 4

Stephen says
- The gradient of line 2 is -1
- (0,2) and (2,0) are both on line 2
- (2,5) is on line 4
- The gradient of line 3 is 2

Ben says
- Gradient of line 1 is 2
- (-2,1) is on line 4
- (0,-3) is on line 4
- (-1,-4) is on lines 3 & 4

Oliver says
- Line 4 would be parallel to y = x
- (0.5,0) is on line 1
- (4,-2) is on line 2
- Gradient of line 3 is 2

WHERE?

The murder took place at the coordinates described by the following.

- It is on the line y = 2x - 5
- The y coordinate is less than the x coordinate
- The sum of the coordinates is 8.5

Draw the line and think about coordinates on the line.

Mark your answer with a large "x"

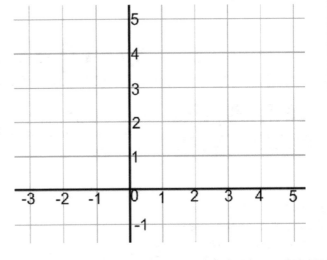

WHY?

Work out these gradients then decode the message below.

A	B	C	D	E
Grad of y = 2x - 1	Grad of y = -4x - 9	Grad of y = 5x + 6	Grad of y = 3x + 1	Grad of y = $\frac{1}{4}$x + 5
F	**G**	**H**	**I**	**J**
Grad of y = 0.6x	Grad of y = x - 1	Grad of y = -3x + 2	Grad of y = 6x - 7	Grad of y = 20x - 10
k	**L**	**M**	**N**	**O**
Grad of y = -1.2x - 1	Grad of y = -2$\frac{1}{2}$x + 5	Grad of y = -2x + 3	Grad of y = 0.5x + 6	Grad of y = -12x + 3
P	**Q**	**R**	**S**	**T**
Grad of y = -x + 8	Grad of y = 8x - 6	Grad of y = 1.5x - 1	Grad of y = 10x	Grad of y = 2.5x + 3
U	**V**	**W**	**X**	**Y or Z**
Grad of y = 3	Grad of y = -0.5x + 1	Grad of y = -7x	Grad of y = 9x + 10	Grad of y = 4x + 5

-4	$\frac{1}{4}$	5	2	0	10	$\frac{1}{4}$	10
-3	$\frac{1}{4}$	6	10	10	4	-2	-2
$\frac{1}{4}$	2.5	1$\frac{1}{2}$	6	5	2	-2.5	

FINAL ACCUSATION

_____ murdered _____

At (coordinate position) _____

Because (why)_____

Mini Murder Mystery 24
Graphs Mix

WHO?

This travel graph shows Sue's journey from home to a friend's house 10km away, and home again. She stopped to buy petrol on the way there.

6 suspects have made statements about Sue's journey. The murderer has made 3 errors and the victim has made none.

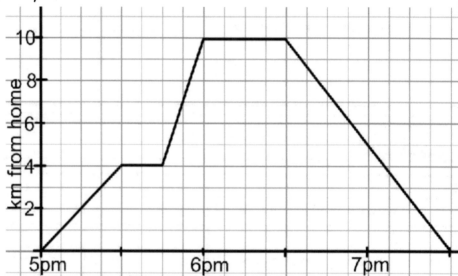

Alex says
- Sue stayed at her friend's house for 30mins
- Her speed on the return journey was 10km per hr
- The return journey is all downhill

George says
- She stopped for 20mins on the way to her friend's house.
- The fastest section of the journey was the first 4km
- Her total journey time was 2½ hrs

Ottilie says
- Sue's speed on the trip from the petrol station to her friend's was 12km per hr
- Sue left her friend's house at 6:20
- It is 10km from the petrol station to Sue's friend's.

Amie says
- Sue spends 15min at the petrol station
- The journey home took 45 mins
- The total journey was 20km

Gregor says
- The average speed for the whole trip was 8km per hr
- Sue was not travelling for 45mins
- At 7pm Sue was half way home

Ruby says
- Sue left the petrol station at 5:45
- From the petrol station to her friend's Sue travelled at 24km per hr.
- At 6:45 Sue was 4km from home.

**WHEN?** The coordinates (-2, 5) and (4, 8) are both on the line
$$y = 0.5x + 6$$
Find the missing coordinate for 4 more points on the same line to find when the murder was committed.

The hour part of the time is the missing x coordinate here. (_____, 10)	The minutes part of the time is the missing y coordinate here. (30, _____)
The day part of the date is the missing x coordinate here. (_____, 10.5)	The month part of the date is the missing y coordinate here. (10, _____)

WHERE? A, B, C are 3 coordinates of the vertices of a quadrilateral.

Some possible coordinates for the 4th position D are given.
The incorrect statement identifies the place where the murder happened.

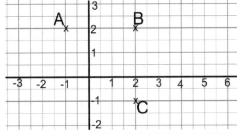

To make a square D is (-1,-1) In Palace Square	To make a parallelogram D is (4,-1) In King Square
To make a trapezium D is (1,-1) In Queen Square	To make a kite D is (-2,-2) In Prince's Square

WHY? Calculate the y coordinate for the curve $y = x^2 + 3x - 10$ for these x coordinates.

A	C	D	E	H	K	N
11	-2	2	5	0	1	12
O	R	U	V	W	Y	
3	6	10	4	-10	-11	

-10	30	0	44	30	60	144	60	8
170	-6	78	-12	120	44	18	30	

FINAL ACCUSATION

_____ murdered _____

On _____ at_____

Because (why)_____

Mini Murder Mystery 25
Units Conversion

WHO? These are the results for 4 children taking part in 5 "events".

6 other pupils have made statements about the results. The murderer has made 3 errors and the victim none.

	welly throw	headstand	walk 100m backwards	shove a penny	exhale 1 breath
Sam	13.4m	2min 15sec	18.5sec	0.6m	290cm^3
Lottie	12.8m	2.5min	16.6sec	45cm	0.5litres
Dee	9.6m	2.25min	20sec	0.44m	0.68litres
Ethan	15.08m	2min 5sec	17.1sec	90mm	580cm^3

Abigail said
- Dee was slowest at walking backwards
- Lottie won the shove a penny
- Ethan exhaled the most air

Joe said
- Dee and Sam did a headstand for the same length of time
- Lottie's shove a penny was 36cm further than Ethan
- Sam came 2nd in the welly throw

Matthew said
- Ethan's welly throw was 3m further than Lottie's
- Lottie's headstand lasted 2min 50 sec
- Sam exhaled the least air

Joshua said
- Dee exhaled 18ml more than Lottie
- The 2 closest welly throws were only 6cm apart
- Ethan was the first to give up on the headstand

Penny said
- The distance between the 2 longest welly throws was over 2m
- The total time spent in headstands was 9.4mins
- Sam was 2.7sec faster at walking backwards than Ethan

Fiona said
- Dee exhaled 0.1 litres more than Ethan
- Lottie was 3.4 secs faster than Dee in the 100m walking backwards event
- Sam shoved a penny 30cm less than Ethan

WHEN?

This conversion graph approximately links ounces to grams.

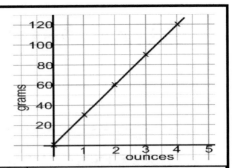

Use it to make the following conversions and find the date of the murder.
(All answers will be integers)

Day change 90g to ounces	Month change 240g to ounces	Year change 67 ounces to g

WHERE?

These tables show the distances in miles and km between 4 towns. The miles distances are all correct. The km distances are not all converted correctly. Decide how many conversions are correct to discover the place of the murder.

miles

	Axbury	Bixton	Degton
Bixton	20		
Degton	32	25	
Henton	16	15	8

km

	Axbury	Bixton	Degton
Bixton	32		
Degton	20	40	
Henton	10	24	5

At the finish line if 3 conversions are correct	At the sand pit if 2 conversions are correct
At the high jump if 1 is correct	At the javelin if 4 conversions are correct

WHY?

Change these times into minutes then decode the murderer's message

A	D	E	H	I	K	L
2.5hrs	0.25hrs	300sec	90sec	2.1hrs	12sec	1hr20min
M	O	Q	R	S	T	U
2hrs10min	1.8hrs	180sec	3.5hrs	3hrs20min	2hrs	1min45sec

1.5	5	200	150	126	15	150	130	126
80	5	5	3	1.75	150	80	200	150
0.2	126	80	108	130	5	120	210	5

FINAL ACCUSATION

_____ murdered _____

On (when) _____ at (where) _____

Because (why)_____

Mini Murder Mystery 26
Volumes

WHO? Here are 3 objects. The suspects have each written 2 statments. The murderer is the person whose statements are incorrect. The victim is the person whose statements are correct.

Cylinder radius = a, height = b	Cube all lengths = a	Cuboid length=a, width =b, height=c
		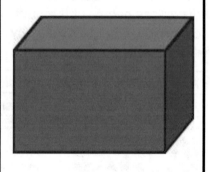

Rebecca says

- The cylinder has the largest volume if a=1,b=2,c=3
- The cuboid has the largest volume if a=10,b=20,c=30

Megan says

- The cuboid has the largest volume if a=0.5,b=1,c=2
- The cube is smallest if a=0.5,b=1,c=2

William says

- The cube has the largest volume if a=3,b=2,c=1
- The cuboid is smallest if a=30,b=20,c=10

Catherine says

- If a=b=c all the shapes will have the same volume
- If a and b are both less than 1 and c is 5,the cuboid will be largest

Jake says
- If a=0.5 and b=c=2.5 the cylinder is largest
- If a and b are both 4 and c is 3.5 , the cuboid is largest

Luke says

- If a, b and c are all 0.5, the cube and cuboid will be identical
- The cube can never be the largest.

WHEN?

The correct formulae indicate the date of the murder.

The volume of this triangular prism can be worked out using one of these 3 formulae:

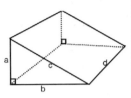

The volume of this prism can be worked out using one of these 3 formulae:

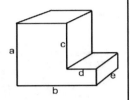

$V=\frac{1}{2}abcd$	$V=\frac{1}{2}abd$	$V=\frac{1}{2}acd$	$V=e(ab+cd)$	$V=(a+b)x(c+d)xe$	$V=e(ab-cd)$
1st Jan	8th Aug	10th Oct	2011	2012	2013

WHERE?

This is a square based pyramid.
The formula for the volume is $v = \frac{1}{3}\pi x^2 h$

If the volume is $9\pi cm^2$ the murder was committed at the pyramids in Giza.

If the volume is $6\pi cm^3$ the murder was committed at the pyramid of the sun in Mexico.

If the volume is $9\pi cm^3$ the murder was committed at the Las Vegas pyramid.

If the volume is $3\pi cm^3$ the murder was committed at the pyramid at the Louvre

calculate the volume when
x=3cm and h=3cm

WHY?

Work out the missing length that would make a cuboid with a volume of 240cm³

A	D	E	H	I	M
10,12,___	40,1,___	24,10,___	24,2,___	0.5,120,___	2.4,10,___
P	R	S	W	Y	
60,0.5,___	5,16,___	4,5,___	2,5,___	2,6,___	

12	5	1	12	2	4	6	2	8	20	3	2
10	4	6	24	2	12	2	8	3	4	12	10

FINAL ACCUSATION

_____ murdered _____

On (Date) _____ at(where) _____

Because (why) _____

Mini Murder Mystery 27
Circles

WHO? Here are 6 circles or parts of circles. Calculate the circumference (or arc length), diameter, radius and the area of each, then study the 6 suspects' statements.
The murderer has made 2 errors, the victim has made none.
In all calculation use 3.14 as π, and round any answers off to 2 dec

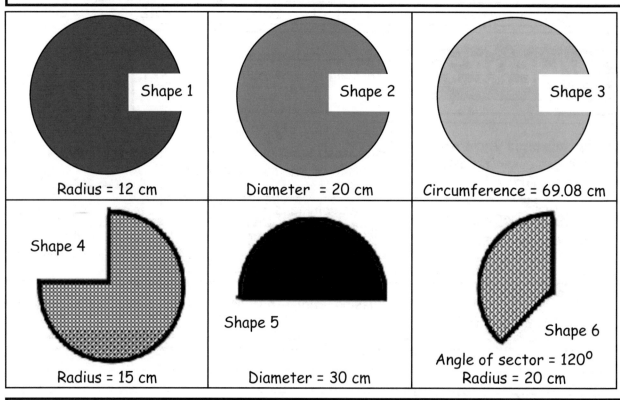

Shape 1 — Radius = 12 cm

Shape 2 — Diameter = 20 cm

Shape 3 — Circumference = 69.08 cm

Shape 4 — Radius = 15 cm

Shape 5 — Diameter = 30 cm

Shape 6 — Angle of sector = 120° — Radius = 20 cm

Ellie says
• The largest area is shape 4
• The radius of shape 3 is 11

Matt says
• Area 5 is greater than area 2
• Arc length of shape 4 is 94.2

Aisling says
• The length of the curve in shape 6 is 41.87
• The area of shape 5 is 1413

Rebecca says
• Shape 2's circumference is 31.4cm
• Shape 6 has the 3rd largest area

Sam says
• Shape 6 is a third of shape 2
• The arc length on shape 4 is 1.5 times as long as the arc length on shape 5

James says
• Shape 3 has the smallest area
• The diameter of shape 1 is 6cm

WHERE? Imagine a circle with a radius of 20cm. These statements are about fractions of that circle and their arc lengths. The false statement tells you where the murder took place.

It was on the London Eye if this is false. A 90° sector has an arc length of 31.4cm.
It was on roundabout if this is false. The arc length of ¾ of the circle is 94.2 cm.
It was in the Leeds Corn Exchange if this is false. A 60° sector has an arc length of 21.1 cm.
It was in the Albert Hall in London if this is false. A semi-circle has an arc length of 62.8 cm.

WHEN? You know that the number pi, π is 3.14. This is the simple rounded off version. It's really a never ending decimal. Here it is written out to 100 decimal places.

3.141 592 653 589 793 238 462 643 383 279 502
884 197 169 399 375 105 820 974 944 592 307
816 406 286 208 998 628 034 825 342 117 067 9...

The hours part of the time is the 52nd dec place.	The minutes part of the time is the 97th and 98th decimal places.
The date is the 60th decimal place.	The month is the 72nd dec place.

WHY? Calculate the **radius** of each of these circles or sectors. Then put them in ascending order to match up with the reason for the murder.

Shape U	Shape V	Shape X	Shape Y	Shape Z
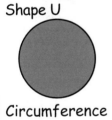				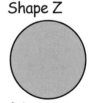
Circumference = 12.56 cm	Area = 113.03cm²	Area = 100.48cm²	Arc length = 10.99cm	Diameter = 10cm

She could only remember pi to 5 decimal places	U, Z, V, X, Y
She called a pair of compasses a compass	U, Z, V, Y, X
She forgot her compasses	U, Z, Y, X, V
She said area was π x diameter	X, Y, V, Z, U

FINAL ACCUSATION

_____ murdered _____

At (place) _____ on (Date) _____ at(time)_____

Because (why)_____

Mini Murder Mystery 28
Shapes & Angles

WHO? The 6 shapes below are not drawn accurately. The 6 suspects have each made 2 statements about them. The murderer has made 2 errors. The victim has made 0 errors.

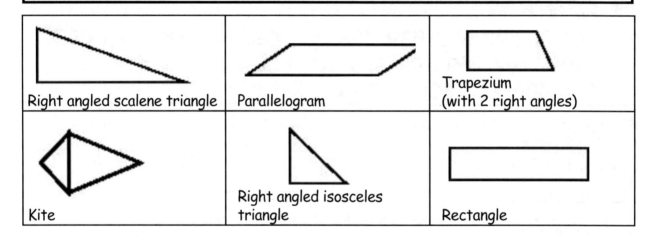

Right angled scalene triangle	Parallelogram	Trapezium (with 2 right angles)
Kite	Right angled isosceles triangle	Rectangle

Matthew says
- The diagonals of 2 of the shapes will cross each other at right angles
- Putting 2 of the right angled scalene triangles together could make a rectangle.

Jade says
- 2 of the shapes have rotational symmetry of order 2
- There are just 2 shapes which contain no equal length edges

Olivia says
- 3 shapes have 2 pairs of parallel edges
- The right angled isosceles triangle is half a square.

James says
- 2 shapes have just 1 line of symmetry
- The diagonals of the parallelogram are the same length as each other

Molly says
- If you joined 2 of the kites together you could make a rectangle
- The parallelogram has reflectional and rotational symmetry

Daniel says
- The right angled scalene triangle is the only shape with no equal angles.
- There are 7 right angles in total

WHEN?

Calculate (don't measure) the marked angles in these regular polygons.

| The hours part is the number of sides on shape A |
| The minutes part of the time is angle b |
| The day is angle c |
| The month is the number of edges shape D will have. |

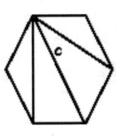

Shape A

b

c

Interior angle = 150°
Shape D
(only part shown)

WHERE?

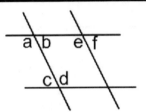

a b   e f

c d

| In Park Square if a and c are alternate angles |
| In Jubilee Square if e and b are corresponding angles |
| In Queens Square if a and d are alternate angles |
| In Kings Square if a and f are corresponding angles |

WHY?

Calculate the 3rd angle in each case to complete a triangle.

100, 45, A	20, 90, C	34, 68, D	90, 80, E	55, 65, H
40, 75, L	10, 10, N	125, 25, O	64, 103, P	36, 54, R
85, 70, S	98, 35, T	81, 35, U		

25	60	10	70	30	64	65	78
160	47	64	25	10	35	13	90
30	47	90	35	70	47	30	90

FINAL ACCUSATION

_____ murdered _____

On (date) _____ At (time) _____ In (place) _____

Because (reason) _____

Mini Murder Mystery 29
Transformations

WHO? The 6 suspects below have each made 3 statements about these transformations. The murderer has made 3 errors. The victim has made no errors.

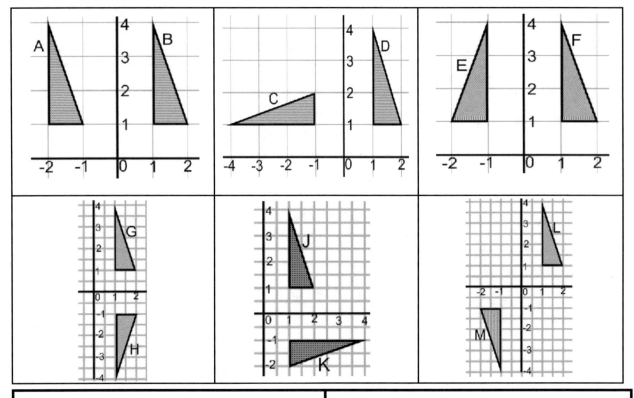

Carl said
- A to B is a reflection in the y axis
- J to K is a rotation of 90° clockwise about (0,0)
- L to M is a reflection in the line y = x

Sanjay said
- G is a reflection of H in the y axis
- D to C is a rotation of 90° clockwise about (0,0)
- B to A is a translation of $\binom{0}{-3}$

Heather said
- C to D is a 90° clockwise rotation about (0,0)
- E to F is a reflection in the line y=0
- G to H is a reflection in the line x=0

Lorna said
- From F to E is a reflection in the y axis
- From C to D is a rotation of 90° clockwise about (0,0)
- A to B is a translation of $\binom{-3}{0}$

Sinead said
- B to A is a translation of $\binom{3}{0}$
- G to H is a reflection in the x axis
- D to C is a rotation of 90° anticlockwise about (0,0)

Frank said
- From J to K is a rotation of 90° clockwise about (0,0)
- L to M is a rotation of 180° about (0,0)
- E is a reflection of F in the y axis

WHERE?

Work out the scale factor for each separate enlargement in this diagram then select the place where the murder happened from the statements below.

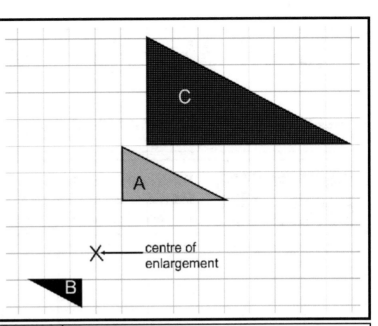

If B – A has sf = 2 it was at the museum	If C - B has sf = 0.25 it was at the concert
If A – B has sf = -2 it was at the art gallery	If C – A has sf = 0.5 it was at the theatre

WHY?

Start in the bottom left corner and follow the translation vectors to spell out the reason.
E.g. The first translation will take you from "start" to "H"

F	E	T	A	P
K	H	C	O	S
START HERE	G	I	R	N

$\binom{1}{1}$ H	$\binom{0}{1}$	$\binom{-1}{0}$	$\binom{3}{-1}$	$\binom{0}{-1}$	$\binom{-2}{0}$
$\binom{2}{1}$	$\binom{-1}{1}$	$\binom{0}{0}$	$\binom{1}{-1}$	$\binom{0}{1}$	$\binom{1}{-1}$
$\binom{-4}{0}$	$\binom{0}{1}$	$\binom{3}{-1}$	$\binom{0}{-1}$	$\binom{-1}{2}$	$\binom{1}{-2}$
$\binom{0}{2}$	$\binom{-1}{-1}$	$\binom{0}{-1}$	$\binom{2}{0}$	$\binom{-3}{0}$	$\binom{3}{2}$
$\binom{-1}{0}$	$\binom{1}{0}$	$\binom{-3}{0}$	$\binom{2}{-2}$	Make sure you always do !	

FINAL ACCUSATION

_____ murdered _____

At (place) _____

Because (Why) _____

Mini Murder Mystery 30
Scattergraphs and Stem & Leaf

WHO?
These scattergraphs show the time spent by 9 students on homework and their results. 6 people have made statements about them. The murderer has made 2 errors, the victim has made none.

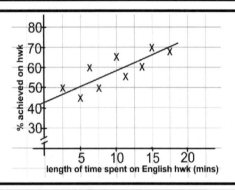
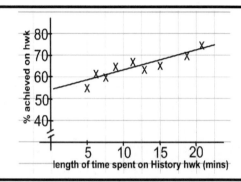

Christopher says
• Both show positive correlation
• The person who did best at English also did best at History

Charles says
• The graphs show that the more time spent on homework, the better the %
• The person who spent 5 mins on English also spent 5 mins on History.

Bea says
• The History graph shows stronger correlation than the English graph
• You can't tell which point is which person

Rebecca says
• The maximum mark for either subject was 80%
• 2 people scored 50% in English

Samantha says
• Both graphs show negative correlation
• The person who scored 60% in English spent 7.5 mins on History

Taneel says
• History's line of best fit shows that if you spend 10 mins you will get just over 60%
• It's impossible to get 80%

WHEN?
Consider whether these would produce positive, negative or no correlation on a scattergraph.

The amount of petrol left in the tank and the number of miles travelled	The amount of glue needed to stick in worksheets and the number of worksheets.
Your level of intelligence and the number of pairs of shoes you own	The % of your income you spend and the % you save

If all are +, it happened at 4pm	If 3 are + it happened at 3pm
If 2 are + it happened at 2pm	If 1 is + it happened at 1pm

WHERE?

This stem & leaf diagram shows the number of texts made by a group of students one day.

Decide how many of the 4 statements are true to decide where the murder happened.

```
2 | 6 6 7 9
3 | 0 1 4 6 8 8
4 | 2 6 7
5 | 0 1
```

An extra pupil made 37 texts. This will raise the median to 37.	An extra pupil made 52 texts. This will raise both the range and median by 1
The pupil who made 47 texts suddenly realises he actually only made 41. This will not affect the median or range at all.	An extra pupil makes 25 texts. This will lower the range and median by 1

If all are true it was in a Maths lesson	If 2 are true it was in an English lesson
If 3 are true it was in a History lesson	If just 1 is true it was in a French lesson

WHY?

Calculate the number that is needed to make the **mean of each set = 8**. Then decode the message below.

A	C	E	H	I	L
5,10,3,___	-10,-10,___	1,1,1,1,1___	3,___	0,1,2,3,4,5,___	30,10,___
N	O	P	R	S	T
24,8,___	12,12,___	8,___	8,9,10,___	0,0,0,___	32,24,16,___

32	13	43	44	14	-8	-40	32
8	43	-16	-16	44	0	5	5
43	-16	14	-40	41	0	-8	

FINAL ACCUSATION

_____ murdered _____

On (when) _____ at (where) _____

Because (why)_____

Mini Murder Mystery 31
Harder Statistical Calculations

WHO? A nature reserve measures the height of 40 saplings. The results are in the table. 6 of the park rangers make some statements. The murderer has made 3 errors, the victim none.

height of saplings (cm)	Freq	midpoint	totals
120 < h ≤ 130	8		
130 < h ≤ 140	14		
140 < h ≤ 150	15		
150 < h ≤ 160	3		

Jack says
- The mean height is 10cm
- The median height is 140cm
- There are more trees over 140cm than under 140cm

Molly says
- The mean is 138.25cm
- 18 trees are > 140cm
- The heights of all the trees add up to 560cm

Maisie says
- The mean is 1382.5cm
- The total height of all the saplings is 5530cm
- There are no trees over 160cm

Derek says
- The mean is 140cm
- The median is in the 130-140cm group
- The modal group is 140-150cm

Edward says
- The mean is 138.25cm
- The modal group is 140 – 150cm
- There are more trees under 130cm than over 150cm

Florence says
- There are no trees under 120
- There are 40 trees in the survey
- The median height tree is in the 140 - 150cm group.

WHEN?

200 students going into an exam were asked how many items were in their clear pencil case.

The results are in the frequency table.

The date and time of the murder is given by

mode = day, median = month
range = hours, mean = minutes

no of items in pencil case	frequency (no of pupils)
10	42
11	24
12	35
13	5
14	3
15	67
16	24

WHERE?

Here is a list of numbers, but 2 are missing. The range of all 6 numbers is 17, the mode is 17, the median is 12 and the mean is 11. Work out the 2 missing numbers

1, __ , 7, 17, __ , 18

If they are 6 & 17 the murder was in Midchester	If the numbers are 5 & 18 the murder was in Midway
If they are 7 & 17 the murder was in Middleton	If the numbers are 11 & 17 the murder was in Midley

WHY?

Calculate the missing value that works out the given mean. Then decode the murderer's message.

A	D	E	H	I
12, 4, 1, __ Mean = 5	100, __ , 98 Mean = 66	__ , 1, 1, 2, 3, 3 Mean = 2	0, 14, 18, __ Mean = 9	6.5, 8.1, 9, 9, __ Mean = 6.6
M	**N**	**O**	**T**	**I**
3.8, 12.9, __ Mean = 8.4	__ , 12, 12 Mean = 10	8, 7, 6, 5, 4, __ Mean = 30	60, 10, __ , 20 Mean = 30	1, 0, 1, 0, 1, 0, __ Mean = 3

0.4	0	0.4	0	6	30	8.5
2	3	6	30	150	0	150
0.4	30	4	3	4	3	18
						!

FINAL ACCUSATION

_____ murdered _____

On (when) _____ at (where) _____

Because (why) _____

Mini Murder Mystery 32
Relative Frequency & Frequency Polygons

WHO?

Six suspects have made some statements about the frequency polygon which shows the number of songs downloaded by the girls and boys in year 9.

The murderer has made 3 errors, the victim has made 0 errors.

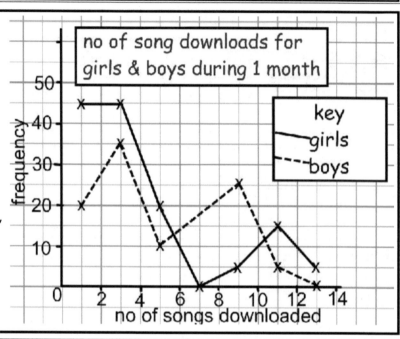

no of song downloads for girls & boys during 1 month

key
girls
boys

frequency

no of songs downloaded

Catherine says
• 10 girls downloaded between 4 & 6 songs
• 1 girl downloaded 45 songs
• 30 pupils downloaded between 8 & 10 songs

Ciaran says
• There are 125 girls
• 25 boys downloaded between 8 & 10 songs
• 5 boys downloaded 10 songs

Fergus says
• The same number of boys & girls downloaded 13 songs
• 10 more boys than girls downloaded between 4 & 6 songs
• 90 girls downloaded ≤ 4 songs

Harriet says
•   There are 125 boys
•   Between 6 & 8 girls downloaded 0 songs
•   5 boys downloaded 10 songs

Polly says
• 55 pupils downloaded over 8 songs
• 0 boys downloaded 13 songs
• There are 220 pupils in year 9

Michael says
• There are 95 boys
• 10 more girls than boys downloaded between 2 & 4 songs
• 20 girls & 20 boys downloaded up to 6 songs

WHEN?

In an experiment to find whether a 6 sided dice was biased the following relative frequencies were calculated

1	2	3	4	5	6
0.11	0.13	0.4	0.21	0.08	0.07

after 120 throws. The correct statement tells you the date.

The dice is not biased because the relative frequencies total 1.	11th Jan	The dice is biased towards 3 as 3 had a higher relative frequency than the rest	13th Feb
The dice is biased towards 4 as it was shaken the most, 21 times.	4th March	The dice is not biased as all the relative frequencies are under a half.	21st April

WHERE?

A sweet was picked from a box containing 40 sweets, the colour

red	green	white	orange	blue
12	50	1	26	11

recorded and the sweet returned. This was done 100 times. Which of the following combinations is most likely to be the number of each type of sweet in the box ?

The murder was committed in the sweet shop if this is most probable

red	green	white	orange	blue
6	25	1	13	5

red	green	white	orange	blue
5	20	1	10	4

The murder was committed in a garden centre if this is most probable.

The murder was committed in a café if this is most probable.

red	green	white	orange	blue
6	20	1	8	5

red	green	white	orange	blue
5	20	0	10	5

The murder was committed in a book shop if this is most probable.

WHY? Make the sets of relative frequencies total 1

A	E	H	I	L	M	O
0.4,0.5,___	___,0.26,0.34	0.8,0.08.___	0.11,0.33.___	0.18.___0.32	0.38,0.28.___	0.27,0.07.___

P	R	S	T	V	Y	
0.09,0.08.___	0.41,0.02.___	0.21,0.4.___	0.2,___,0.05	___0.71,0.09.	___,0.6,0.1.	

0.39	0.12	0.4	0.56	0.39	0.34	0.3	0.57	0.4	0.5
0.1	0.75	0.56	0.2	0.4	0.83	0.66	0.5	0.5	0.3

FINAL ACCUSATION

_____ murdered _____

On (when) _____ at (where) _____

Because (why) _____

Answers

Task	Murderer	Victim	When	Where	Reason
17	Lucy	Lydia	5pm. Sat 5th March 2013	The charity shop	She ate sixty percent of my chips
18	Phil	Janet	28/9/2012 at 5:43	Southampton	She thought dec pl meant decide pleased !
19	Alex	Adam	Oct 10th 2010	Swansea	Because he was so powerful
20	Hollie	Sam	$\frac{1}{4}$ past 2 pm on 31.3.2011	Ice Hockey match	He said ten squared was twenty
21	Beth	Amy	9:15 on 6th December	Dining Room	She wrote a straight x not a curly one
22	Lena	Ciaran	2nd February 2002	At the roundabout	He said sequences were hard !
23	Lucy	Chloe		(4.5, 4)	Because she is symmetrical
24	Ottilie	Gregor	8:21 on 9th November	King Square	He drew a wonky curve
25	Penny	Joe	3rd August 2010	At the finishing line	He said a mile equals a kilometre
26	Jake	Megan	8th August 2013	Las Vegas Pyramid	She said a pyramid was a prism
27	James	Ellie	8:06 on 4th June	Leeds Corn Exchange	She called a pair of compasses a compass
28	Molly	Jade	8:45 on 30th December	Queens Square	She couldn't use a protractor
29	Sanjay	Frank	1pm	The theatre	He forgot to ask for tracing paper
30	Samantha	Bea	1pm	English lesson	She can't spell correlation
31	Jack	Edward	6:13 on 15th December	Midchester	I didn't mean to do it ha ha !
32	Harriet	Polly	13th February	Garden Centre	She is my relative Polly